TRAUMA BONDING IS NOT FOR ME!!!

People I have met along my path of life & healing – Ashley A. Lenartson

Nanette Mary Michaud-Lenartson she was my mother but she kept a messy house her whole life as she definitely didn't want to become a Professional Singer. The woman could sing and I only ever heard her sing once in my lifetime and I wanted to record what she was singing but I never got the chance to record the song she was singing as I didn't want to interrupt her. It was a song I've never heard before and I'll never know what the song was as I can only imagine that a man wrote the song but who knows who wrote the song: I didn't think to ask her who wrote the song so I'll never know. When she burned her home down to the ground and claimed it was an accident I said, "What are you going to do for an encore???" There was no response from the woman. She was a lazy sloth who just couldn't get her act together and I suspect it was because of her upbringing: she was raped by an Uncle but who hasn't had trauma in their life???

Nanette, Rose & Carl Lenartson, New York

Nanette Mary Michaud Lenartson
Circa 1958
20 years of Age

**Adrian & Delia Brandt-Michaud,
Eagle Lake, Maine**

George H. Michaud he was raised in a totally dysfunctional family in Northern Maine. They were known for being a**holes. That's the rumor I heard. However, when I met his parents they weren't so Polly Pissy Pants: they'd calmed down quite a bit. I knew that the grandfather was depressed and he would sit in his chair and watch t.v. drinking a beer. Delia was a beotch and she didn't like my twister, Rosy, as she didn't like the fact that she was always out w/ her friends getting stoned or drunk and walking the railroad tracks of Eagle Lake, Maine in

George Henry Michaud's 1ˢᵗ Gravestone

Aroostook County in Northern Maine. Such is life. I liked George's parents but I knew they were fucked up but when I met them they seemed pretty "normal" whatever that means. George had a problem w/ his eyes and was not able to see any colors except green, red, black and white and grays. He was once asked to pick blueberries in a field and came back with an empty bucket. He got hell for that. George was a Narcissist thru and thru. It showed in his every move towards his whole family. Nobody liked dealing with or working with George H. Michaud. His wife Nanette was an asskisser and the relationship grew tired and she stopped putting out. How could she do that??? He had a 12" penis I would have gladly sucked off regularly but sadly he was a miserable alcoholic who worked all of the time despite his upbringing and he liked to work as it kept his mind off his problems. He was as straight as they come. So was my mother. My mother never acknowledged my sexuality: why would she want to??? She was always trying to get me to date women, not men. What's up with that??? My mother just sat on her fat ass and thought she was "The Queen". And, she liked putting on make up to make herself look like Cleopatra from Egypt. Maybe she WAS Cleopatra in a previous lives: U just never know about these things! My parents could have reconciled the relationship but only if they had worked on getting along with each other. Sadly, the case was not to be. Some people just don't want to get their act together. It showed with the messy house she kept. He put up with it: I can't put up with a messy house and sadly I've become just like both of my parents but no need to get into the details of that situation I've created for myself!!!

George Henry Michaud - February 1958

George's Final Resting Place, Eagle Lake Cemetary, 2014

Ashley A. Lenartson/Michaud I was born July 21, 1963 @ 3:27AM. My twister, Rosy, was born at 3:17AM. Why do I know these things??? Because I pay attention to dates that are important to me. I was relentlessly picked on by George while I was growing up all over the world. I started becoming a pervert at the young age of _ _. I preferred boys who liked getting their dicks sucked. My first experience was great except I didn't know what I was doing and promptly choked on a boy who was my age's cock and that was that. I'm known as a faggot in Eagle Lake, Maine but what do I care??? It's not my problem if guys don't like sucking cock or taking it deep in their blown out, mangled, jangled beef

curtains.

Ashley Michaud-Lenartson – Eagle Lake, Maine

That's not for me to decide. They can go fuck their girlfriends who have mangled, jangled, blown out beef curtains. I was the one who won awards all the time in Grammar School and still have them to this day. I also rarely missed school unless it was for a great reason like being sick or going somewhere important. I'm considered very smart and know how to produce my own pop music for sale all over the planet. I even know how to master a complete album of Pop Tunes: I'd say that that's pretty impressive. I also know what people are like: needy & greedy so why deal w/ people anymore??? Why! Why! Why! I'm all about not being "trauma bonded" anymore: when somebody starts their ship with me I say, "You need to look up those two words online." I never hear back from them ever again. I just don't have any more time for dramazine! Dramazine sounds like a magazine or a really great drug. But, alas, it's not!!! It's not a good thing like Martha Stewart says: she's right! I'm a solid B++ student which means that I have the capacity for much higher learning

Ashley Michaud Lenartson – Eagle Lake, Maine

Ashley & Sharon early 1980s

Sharon Rose Lenartson/Michaud she's my twin-sister but she was the one who was put on the dais and as a result I've had to battle with her my whole life and that's HER issue, not mine. She thinks that she's better than me and that I'm the shame of the family. Who does she think she is??? I guess her shit doesn't stink. I know mine does!!! She's also very smart but what do I care about a sister who can't respect her brother? She can pretend to dominate me all she wants: I just don't have time for her bullshit.

She can go love her self.

Ashley, Sharon & Michael Michaud – Eagle Lake Elementary School 1977

Sharon-Rose Michaud Lenartson, Elementary School Picture, Eagle Lake, Maine

Sharon-Rose Michaud Lenartson, High School, Fort Kent Community High School, Fort Kent, Maine

She has a degree in Communications but she doesn't use it except to shit all over me. She wants people to think that her shit doesn't stink and that she's filthy rich but the problem with that is that she pays no taxes and works as a migrant worker on a farm taking care of the Organic Vegetables in the field.

What's a girl to do??? Not one of her boyfriends has ever worked out. She is a dominant "Alpha Female Narcissist". I simply don't have time to be controlled by her. She tried to control me when I was younger as she wanted to be my mother but I honestly don't need a mother telling me what to do or fucking up my life. One of her boyfriends kicked her out of his house and refused to give her stuff back to her. I wonder what went down w/ the two of them? Hmmm…

Ashley & Sharon, Peaks Island, Portland, Maine

Michael George Henry Michaud my brother Mickey as I like to call him can't deal with being called Mickey Mouse: what's up with that??? No sense of humor whatsoever! He has a degree in Forestry from The University of Maine at Orono. He doesn't like telling people what to do as it's a big headache according to him. He has a wife by the name of Anne Ludwig-Michaud and they have two children, Andrew Michaud-Ludwig and Margaret Michaud-Ludwig. Andrew has Downs Syndrome and I once sent them a letter saying I don't have a problem w/ retards but should have not used that word. Do U think he could have called me out on it??? I had to hear it from my mother. Lame, lame, lame people are!!! I thought my brother was smarter than me but it turns out that he's not. But, it's not about being smart: **it's about what one can offer the world that matters.**

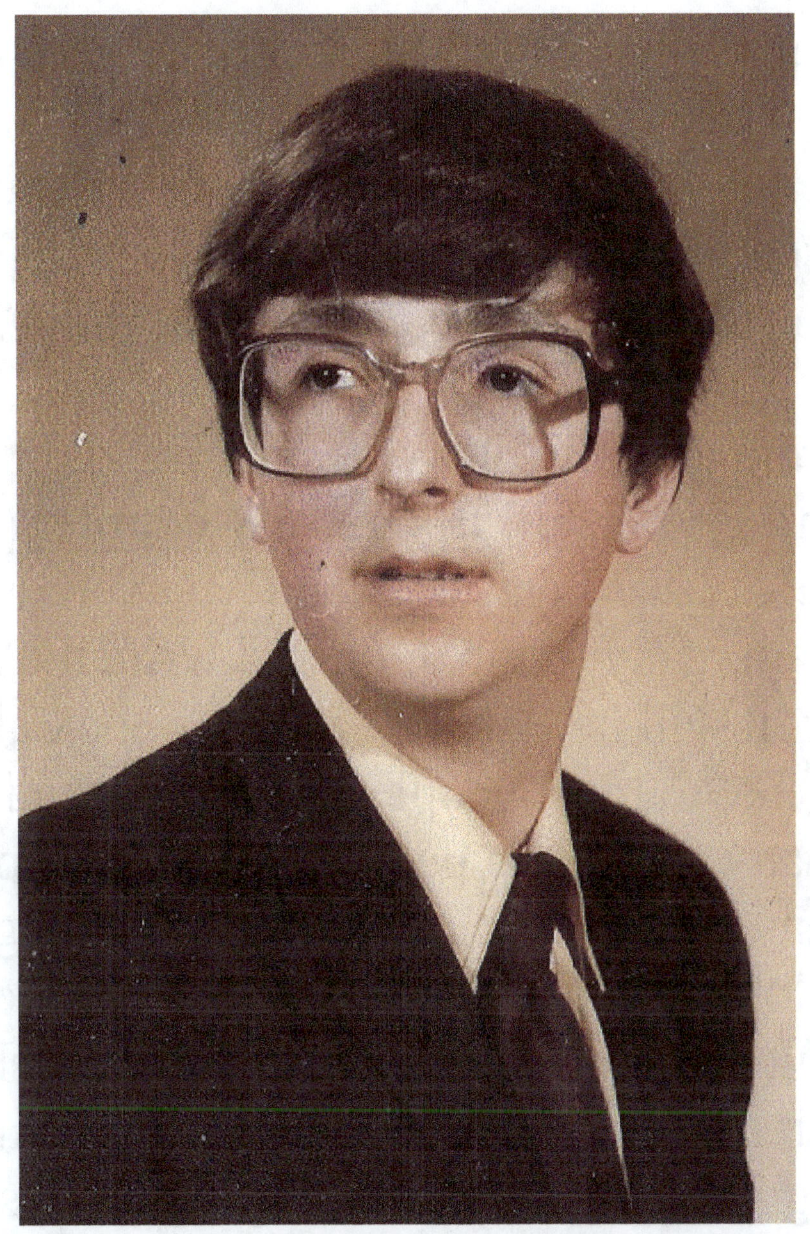

Michael George Michaud, High School, Fort Kent High School 1980

We are all connected. His wife was a Massage Therapist for a very long time but she decided to quit that and get 3 jobs and is tired all the time because she doesn't take care of herself when it comes to her diet. What's a girl to do? Mickey also has a big penis as I saw it one time when I was a teenager. Just like his father has a big dick. What's a boy to do??? I'm obsessed with having a b.f. who has a really big penis. If it's not **BIG** what's the point???

I come from a totally chaotic, dysfunctional family and I don't give a shit: **it's not my problem anymore**: at least I can say that I've overcome my past and am ready to move on and write the rest of this book. It will be Part 1 of a 5 part book about what it's like to meet people who are fucked up. I've met so many fucked up people and been ripped off by so many fucked up people where do I begin??? You'd think that I can learn to separate myself from thieves but I'm not sure: the lesson always shows up in a different form…The best part of my childhood was being **ALONE** a lot and keeping to myself. I always kept myself **BUSY**. It's the only way to live your life: **BUSY, BUSY, BUSY!!!** I always seem to choose people who don't talk much about themselves and who have emotional problems. What's a boy to do??? Nothing except stop choosing people who are so emotional and fucked up!!! I guess it has everything to do with my Emotional

Cancer Nature and my upbringing with being picked on by an "Alpha Male Narcissist Step-Father" who was mad at his parents for treating him the way they did while he was growing up.

They say U can't remember anything below the age of 7 because you're in a different vibration that's called "Theta Brain Waves": why is it then that I have friends who have memories below the age of 7 years of age? Maybe I just chose to block out all the trauma I experienced growing up all around the world and not being able to put down roots and bond with people: maybe that's one of my life lessons that allows me to be the person I have become. Who knows. Believe it or not, "I LOVE PEOPLE and talking to them." It's something I specialize in doing!!! It makes me HAPPY!!! Should have become a Clinical Psychologist!!! I'm always ANALyzing people and the world: it's FFUN FFUN FFUN!!!

Places I've lived New York City – General Population, Albany, New York: Air Force Base, Derby Kansas: Air Force Base, Eagle Lake Maine – General Population, Kaiserslautern, Germany: Air

Force/Army Base Portland, Maine, Old Orchard Beach, Maine: General Population.

Most of my trauma happened in Northern Maine, Aroostook County Maine. I'm **the Black Sheep of the Family** and why should I care? Who likes that title??? Nobody!!! <u>**The Family Reject**</u>: why should that bother me at this point in my life: no thanks to all of that negativity. The best thing to do is get away from people who are damaged and who want to inflict more damage on U or other people: who needs that???

What was my best memory of living in Northern Maine as a child and young adult??? Going out to slide down the hill in the back yard on top of the crusty ice without falling thru as I was so young and not frail. That was FFUN and I did it all by myself. As a matter of fact, I've never felt that comfortable around people which is why I've always preferred to be a LONER and keep to myself. I love listening to American Top 40 and dreaming of the day my stuff gets played on the radio and have 13 albums of pop music to finish and the next album will be a Pop/Rock/Progressive Outfit w/ a pianist, drummer

and guitarist. That's all that I really need right along
w/ me singing along w/ the band. It'll be FFUN
FFUN FFUN and the best thing I've ever done with
my life. I used to perform Stand Up Comedy but
don't know if I'll ever go back to doing that as
people really love me for making them laugh:
laughter makes U forget that U have any problems,
etc. It's relief from your life. Think about it!

What is my earliest memory? Living in Derby,
Kansas on a long street in a rented blue house:
believe me, it gets cold in Derby, Kansas even
though it's the Midwest. There are tornados in
Derby, Kansas thanks to the plains being mostly flat.

People I have met along the way: There are too
many people I've met along the way. I've definitely
never fallen in love with a person and had a
relationship that worked out. I don't know if it's
gonna happen in this life. My main objective is to
overcome being a **REJECT** and people who do this
kind of shit to me are losers and have a big giant
stick up their ass: it's called **"Trauma Bonding"**
which I have no time for anymore: I've simply let
too many people take advantage of me either

because of kindness or shame issues: it's my Cancer Nature so why let anybody take advantage of me? Not gonna happen anymore: I just don't have time for "trauma drama" as it's highly toxic and it can kill or get U killed because 85% of the human race chooses this way of life to learn their lessons. I just have time for better things to happen in my life.

Who is the best person I've ever met? Priscilla Daigle who taught disadvantaged teenagers at Fort Kent High School for many years: she really knew how to work with mentally challenged teenagers and was also an Art Teacher. She knew her stuff. I had drawings that I made as a child but don't know where those landed. Most likely in the trash.

Who's the worst person I've ever met??? 5 boys in Deering Oaks who broke my nose in 1984. They can all rot in hell for being homophobic boys who secretly want to suck cock and take it in the ass. The next day this guy named Mark came up to me in Monument Way and started harassing me and saying, "You're the faggot I beat up in Deering Oaks last night." I said, "If U go away I'll let this go," but he insisted on harassing me and a cop happened to be driving his cop car down the street past the monument in monument way so I stopped him and told him what happened. They arrested Mark and he ended up going to The Correctional Center in South Portland, Maine until he was 21. He deserved what he got and he's lucky somebody hasn't broken his nose yet: it could still happen. He's a piece of shit and scum who used to look like a pretty boy and that's what he couldn't handle about himself besides the fact that his mother threw him out of the house at the age of 14. I was 21 when this happened. It has totally changed my ability to sing the way I know how to sing but that's life. He never ratted the other 4 boys who held me down on the bridge in Pickle Park or The Lonely Hearts Club Band so he could break my nose and push it to the left. He's right handed and definitely a Closet Case who likes taking in both of his holes. What a group of losers. Society teaches people to be homophobic . I'm not buying into this bullshit. I simply don't have time for it. If you're homophobic then why??? Have U thought thru what your hate does to people who are born gay??? Live And Let Live, I say! People who are bullied are more likely to commit suicide and it's the young ones who pay the price. Fuck the world and what it tells U u should be or not be: live your life anyways…

If the people who keep showing up in your life are people who are negative, self-effacing and generally a nuisance then U need to think about the vibration that U put out to the world as that's what is attracting this kind of behavior: change the vibration and U will get a better result. U don't want people in your life who are bringing U down, U want people who support your every move and who make sure that U do succeed with your life as well as with theirs. If people keep bringing U down, don't enable them and get rid of them so that U have no drama in your life. You don't need "trauma bonding" going on with anybody. And, anybody who has taken advantage of U in this life will be energetically dealt with in the next life. From what I know "we live forever" so why worry about anything? Just live the best life that U can live and don't worry about anybody or anything: just don't keep up the pattern of letting people abuse U and take advantage of U because you don't need that in your life. Letting people take advantage of you is not the way to be AFFIRMED by anybody: it just isn't. So, don't do it??? You'll stop doing it when U stop allowing the behavior to happen to you! You're better than that!!!

Helen Hall & Andrea Turner: **1.** False Police Report **2.** Entrapment **3.** Perjury Under Oath EVIL BITCHES: after all, the Po Po never arrested me. So, who can be telling the truth here??? The person who was supposed to help me thru the process of talking to a Bench Judge by the name of Deborah F. Cashman who clearly didn't do her job. What a bitch! A judge can't accept evidence if there is NONE! I can have the case thrown out legally using a lawyer if I want to but to find a lawyer who isn't greedy is the key here. I can also sue the State of Maine for a lot of money as I was "falsely prosecuted for a crime that's not my fault as I didn't initiate said crime." It's impossible to assault a nasty, negative OLD BITCH who is ordering me to do so towards the end of the argument because she has apparently done this kind of behavior to people before: she's an EVIL BITCH, not a WITCH: a witch would know how to use their power for good, not EVIL!

Carolyn Silvius: the old bitch who "claims" to want to go back to Law School to study law but won't. She threw me under the bus: she could have told me how to act in front of the judge but did she? Hell to the NO!!! Fuck Her! That's not a friend. I could have said, "Will U please tell me what to say," but did I??? So, ultimately it's my fault but when U have information and **WITHOLD** it from helping somebody that's called **WITHOLDING**: a very selfish thing to do to someone I say. People do this kind of shit all the time. It's not permissible in my world as I like to be UPFRONT with people, not evil and despicable. That's somebody else's job.

John Mitchell and Charlotte Tumor: borrowed money they never paid back.

Jeff Degallery: chronic drug addict always borrowing money from me like a little child who needs love from his parents. He did pay me back but who needs money leeches in their life??? I certainly don't. One must learn to say, "NO, NO, NO!!!" to people who are INSOLVENT: it's not your problem. Just walk away!

Donald Foster: Slumlord of the Century

Stanley Mortimer & Steven Mortimer: both serious drug addicts and con-artists not to be believed. They'll rip anybody off including their mother!

I can't think of anything to write about today so I guess this is it for now. Maybe tomorrow I'll get the information I need from my brain. Apparently I have an emotional block going on. We're moving gradually from 3D healing to 5d healing: who would have thunk it???

Most of the people I've met in my life have traumatized me in one way or another: I'll have to make a list and say what they did to me that traumatized me: I guess that one of my major life lessons is "overcoming trauma from people who traumatized me".

Just because you are kind to somebody doesn't give U a right to be abusive to that person: either you're going to be kind to that person without expecting anything in return or you're going to not be kind to that person and let them find their

way in their life. You are not required to do anything for anybody unless it's out of the kindness of your heart!

People who have traumatized me: a drunk guy, Mark Varanelli and Mona Liebold, Donald Foster, Jeffrey Grant, Jeff DeGallery, Jeffrey Grants friend Mike, Tim Nickerson, Helen Hall and Andrea Turner, Mike "The Homophobe" Wilbur as in "Wilbur THE Pig", Ryan Belanger, Peggy Watson, Lisa Dixon, Sarah Rowell, Three homeless guys, a homeless woman, a few men who had anger/rage issues, the two boys who lived on Sawyer Street here in Portland, Maine, Troy Dorr: threw the key to my Subaru in the woods so that I would end up having to make a new key for the car. There are so many people I just can't remember all of them. The Incident At Coyle Street, etc. etc. etc.

I was raised in a chaotic and dysfunctional home as my mother was not present unless she had to be present while I was growing up all over the world: she cared more about buying things she didn't need than keeping a clean house. My step-father was the one who married her and he kept himself busy all the time thru work. My mother just sat on her fat ass taking care of 3 children as that was her job and she did try to get a job as an AVON seller but that didn't work out: she ended up with a chest full of AVON products that she never sold: the stuff should have been sold instead of sitting in a chest in the Master Bedroom of my parents' home in Eagle Lake, Maine: a complete waste of money, time and effort.

My twin-sister, Rosy, got away from the family as a teenager and became a party girl with her friends and she had a lot of boyfriends and that's how she dealt with her issues. I escaped into listening to the radio WDHP 96.9 Presque Isle, Maine radio station which played mostly pop rock music. When I discovered American Top 40 with Casey Kasem one day on a Saturday morning I was in heaven and that became the program I listened to all of the time on the weekends two days in a row from start to finish four hours each day: it was FFUN!!! During the week I'd just listen to the station and the Pop Music they played from the 70's. I even made radio tapes but some of the tapes I made were on Certron Tapes which are cheap and the oxides on the tape rub off on the tape machine so I ended up throwing out a case of tapes that had some excellent cassettes with quality tapes in the trash and what I should have done was go thru the tapes to figure out which ones were of quality vs. crappy tapes and saved those. That was a big loss for me but now that we have You Tube and many other music services online all I have to do is hook up a tape machine to the back of my computer and press RECORD to get the songs I lost. I can even DIGITALLY DOWNLOAD the songs I loved from the 70's and save them into my computer which would be the easier way to do it but I happen to love music on tape as then I can play a tape machine and use headphones to listen to the stuff from the digital radio online. Personally, I'm sick of waiting a whole week to listen to and record old American Top 40 Broadcasts from the 80's. I want to record stuff from the 70's as that's the era I listened to most Pop Music from 1975-1981. I remember the 1st songs I ever heard on the radio: Volarie – Dean Martin, Bang, Bang, I Shot My Baby Dead – Sonny & Cher, Uncle Albert/Admiral Halsey – Paul McCartney, Here You Come Again – Dolly Parton, I Feel Love – Donna Summer: the list of pop songs I fell in love with goes on from there. Can't wait to hook up my tape deck to the back of my

ACER Predator Computer and get to taping stuff off You Tube a.s.a.p.

You can't **ass u me** nothin' bout nobody: that's what I learned from a friend of mine by the name of Jeff DeGallery the one who was constantly borrowing money from me: he def. used Sex As A Weapon - Pat Benatar on me and that's not a good thing to do to anybody: he was def. a user: I'm so glad we're not friends anymore: who needs somebody who only cares about your bank account??? That's what Society teaches women to do to men: no wonder we die at much younger ages than women do. And, their best friends are alcohol and drugs??? I don't need that bullshit. Put out or get out! No more handouts of money or anything physical: fuck that! I'm done!

Anonymous 99 Portland, ME in a few seconds

the only person left to L-O-V-E: sweet, wonderful LOVABLE U: go love urself: I know some will substitute the word fk w/ lv butt butt butt dats nawt mi intention: I do mean it: LOVE is all there really is isn't that TRUE: yes, it's TRUE: if love isn't enough U mite want to think things thru about What Love Means To You: I know, I know: Everywhere...

<u>**Let's face it**</u>: Life is one big trauma after the next caused by your mouth or somebody else's mouth: the best U can do is "keep your mouth shut," and #2. Don't Take Anything Personally (Or You'll End Up Regretting It): The Five Agreements. Be Prepared like a Girl Scout or a Boy Scout: just do your homework and be prepared for anything good to happen in your life and Happy Go Lightly!!!

I don't have any pets so I don't have any peeves: Agreement 2. Don't Take Things Personally - The 5 Agreements; as it was never about U it was about their need to <u>**CONTROL YOU**</u>: a narcissist: trauma bonding I seriously don't need. So what did they do??? They made U feel less than!!! Get out of the relationship w/ that person sexual or otherwise if U want your "emotional freedom". And, the next time U see this person or people: don't sit near them, don't engage, just leave: Do U want PEACE or do U need to be right all the time??? This is no way to live your life: go now: do the right thing!

The 7 Stages of Trauma Bonding

Published: August 29, 2022 Updated: November 28, 2022

It has been suggested that there are seven stages of trauma bonding, with each stage perpetuating the cycle of trauma and pain commonly seen in abusive relationships. While it can become increasingly difficult for the victim to walk away from this vicious cycle, it is still possible to break a trauma bond, especially once you are familiar with its stages and how they impact you and your relationship.

What Is Trauma Bonding?

Trauma bonding happens when an abuser uses manipulation tactics and cycles of abuse to make the victim feel dependent on them for care and validation, causing a strong attachment or bond. This often occurs in romantic narcissistic relationships, but can also occur in families, friendships, or work relationships.

Trauma bonding in a relationship can coincide with any physical or sexual abuse that may be present. But whether the abuse is purely psychological or a combination of the two, it may feel impossible to simply "walk away" even when you are being harmed. It can take survivors a long time to find the tools to detach themselves from their trauma bond, and often they stay longer than they should out of fear for their safety or livelihood, which can lead to even worse instances of abuse before they can break free.

Who Is More Susceptible to Trauma Bonding?

People with relational and emotional trauma are typically targeted by perpetrators in a trauma bond, intentionally or otherwise. It can be common for abusers to seek out strong, driven, educated, and independent thinkers so that they can make themselves feel superior when they finally break them down.

Other risk factors for trauma bonding include:

People with dependent personalities

Anyone who puts a lot of value on "the good times" and is quick to forgive

Anyone with a history of being abused in childhood or past relationships

People with disorganized, anxious, or avoidant attachments

People with the tendency to question themselves, even despite strong evidence that suggests they aren't to blame

Existing mental health concerns, such as depression, BPD, and anxiety

People with separation anxiety

People who are sensitive to rejection

On an intellectual level, trauma bond survivors likely know what is happening to them is wrong and can identify how painful and soul-crushing their relationship is. Still they often struggle to accept it as abuse.

Healing from traumatic, abusive relationships isn't easy, but a professional help can make all the difference. **BetterHelp** has over 20,000 licensed therapists who provide convenient and affordable online therapy. **BetterHelp** starts at $60 per week.

Complete a brief questionnaire and get matched with the right therapist for you.

Choosing Therapy partners with leading mental health companies and is compensated for marketing by BetterHelp

Visit BetterHelp

7 Stages of Trauma Bonding

In the seven proposed stages of trauma bonding, often they begin as seemingly excellent relationships before gradually progressing turning into an abusive dynamic. This progression is part of the reason this bond can profoundly impact a victim's worldview, perception of reality, and their relationship with themselves.

The seven stages of trauma bonding are:

1. Love Bombing

Love bombing involves the sudden, intense attempt to create a "we" in a relationship through high praise and excessive flattery. While this dynamic typically occurs between a perpetrator and victim of abuse, it can sometimes involve other people surrounding the couple. Sometimes, in some abusive circumstances, the abuser may seem oblivious to their manipulation; however, that is typically not the case in a trauma bond.

In a trauma bond, love bombing can subtly set the stage for an abusive dynamic by:

Allowing the abuser to prey on the victim's emotions, deep hopes, desires and dreams. It is similar to someone saying "look what I can offer you, and no one else has or will love you like this"

Causing the victim to let their guard down and trust the abuser's intentions

Fostering positive feelings and validation between the possible perpetrator and victim

"Proving" that an abuser has good intentions

Providing a sense of stability and security

2. <u>Trust & Dependency</u>

In this stage, an abuser may purposefully test the victim's trust and dependency on them usually leading to the target feeling guilty for questioning their partner. Doubts are expected in a healthy relationship and it takes time to get to know someone–not only for what they say but also for what they do.

When confronting the abuser at this stage, you may get a lot of flak for discounting all they have done for you, which is why the love bombing stage provides a vital setup for dependency. In trauma bonds, the idea that you can trust an abuser in the relationship is an illusion.

3. Criticism

Once they've got your trust, emotional abusers may start to pick apart some of your qualities, identifying them as insignificant or problematic. This criticism can feel sudden, especially after experiencing the love bombing stage, but it is common for abusers to wait until a victim's trust has been tested before they begin criticizing them.

The criticism phase is most noticeable during intense arguments or disagreements, where the abuser will likely blame their partner and the target may end up over-apologizing for things that are not their fault.

They may start to think along the lines of:

"Wow, he still loves me and forgives me, even when I mess up."

"You're right, I'm so sorry for questioning you."

"You want what's best for me, so you're right."

This back-and-forth dance of harsh criticism and over-apologizing is the glue forming the trauma bond.

4. Manipulation & Gaslighting

Gaslighting and manipulation are two forms of psychological abuse often seen in trauma bonds that ultimately make victims question their reality and perception. Gaslighters will never fully or honestly take responsibility for their behaviors, and tend to shift blame onto the other person. It is very common for gaslighters to suddenly seem calm, cool, and collected once they have pushed their target to their breaking point. Gaslighting is a textbook behavior among common types of abusers like narcissists, sociopaths, and psychopaths.

Fighting back or challenging the abuser can often feel like it will never result in anything good, which sometimes leads to reactive abuse by the target. This term refers to the seemingly abusive behaviors committed by the target towards the oppressor out of blinding rage, survival or psychological preservation. **1.** It is normal for victims who engage in reactive abuse to feel extremely guilty and concerned when their behavior turns physical, leading the target of abuse to further question their identity, primarily because the gaslighting type of abuser seeks to isolate the target from anything and anyone that gives them a sense of reassurance, normalcy or independence.

5. <u>Resignation & Giving Up</u>

When dealing with a trauma bond, it is very common for targets of abuse to start giving in at some point to avoid more conflict. The "fawn" trauma response, or bargaining and people-pleasing behaviors, may ensure the relationship can remain somewhat stable. **3.** Targets may have some awareness they are being manipulated, but that small awareness may not be enough to exit the relationship yet, because the target may still be questioning whether or not they are to blame for the abuser's behavior.

Depending on the length of the relationship and the nature of the psychological abuse, a target often becomes more dependent on the abuser to avoid further conflict by getting married, having children, or becoming more emotionally and financially reliant on their partner. There are many reasons why an abused person cannot easily leave, including safety concerns. It is natural to fear that an abuser's behavior may escalate when they sense they are losing control when a target is threatening to leave or actually walking out of the door. Things can escalate and become physical or deadly for many domestic disputes.

6. Loss of Self

Throughout the stages of a trauma bond, there is a progressive loss of self, which brings tremendous pain and a disconnection from the world we once knew. People who leave abusive relationships may not seem like their usual selves due to a loss of their own identity and personal boundaries. **4.** Trauma bonds can be incredibly isolating, as you can lose many of your social connections due to the changes of self-identity that no longer match what people close to you are used to. This level of psychological destruction may lead to a complete loss of confidence and even suicidal ideation. For many, this emotional torture, shame, and guilt is built up for years, which can make it very difficult to face and move forward from.

7. Addiction to the Cycle

Often in trauma bonds, the stages can be cyclical; after a significant conflict, there may be a cool down or honeymoon period. At this moment of peace, the abuser might apologize and start the love-bombing process all over again, which makes the target feel relieved and desired, thus positively reinforcing a dependency on this abusive cycle.

Conversely, the abuser may completely shut down, become avoidant, and withhold all love, affection, and attention as a way to pressure or force the victim to apologize. When the responsibility and blame become pinned on the target, they may go to extremes to gain back favor from their abuser. By doing so, the target is falsely given the sense that they have control, and they may draw conclusions that the abuser must really love them when they succeed at winning them back, reinforcing the idea that the victim is to blame.

Help For Trauma / PTSD

Talk Therapy – Get help recovering from trauma from a licensed therapist. Betterhelp offers online therapy starting at $60 per week. Get matched With A Therapist.

Virtual Psychiatry – Get help from a real doctor that takes your insurance. Talkiatry offers medication management and online visits with top-rated psychiatrists. Take the online assessment and have your first appointment within a week. Free Assessment.

Guided Psychedelic Journeys – Ketamine is a prescription medication that clinicians can prescribe off-label to treat trauma, depression, anxiety, and OCD. Innerwell pairs ketamine with support from licensed psychotherapists. Find out if you're a good candidate: Take Online Assessment

Choosing Therapy partners with leading mental health companies and is compensated for marketing by BetterHelp, Talkiatry, and Innerwell.

What Do These Stages Do to the Brain?

Research suggests that exposure to trauma confuses or shocks the brain and may lead to several biological changes and stress responses, including post-traumatic stress disorder (PTSD), other mental illnesses, substance use disorders, changes in the limbic system, changes in hormones, altered brain chemistry, as well as decreases in brain functioning. Some of these changes may be internal and, therefore, more difficult to notice.

Additional impacts of trauma on the brain may include:

5. Developing chronic illnesses

Overt displays of emotional distress, such as panicking

Internal reactions, like dissociation

Fatigue

Brain fog

Sleep issues (i.e., nightmares, insomnia, etc)

Fear of recurrence

Flashbacks

Avoidance

How to Break Free From Trauma Bonding

When trying to break free from a trauma bond or abusive situation, it is ideal to have immediate access to a support system or direct phone support via a reputable hotline to help manage difficult and confusing moments. Making a plan with your support system to leave quietly or conflict-free while your abuser is away may help you get out of the door and stay as safe as possible, as the act of leaving is statistically the most dangerous point in abusive relationships.

1,5. **When to Seek Therapy**

Therapy can be a great addition to your support system, and there are specific trauma-based therapy practice, such as Trauma-Focused CBT, that specialize in working with survivors of abuse. You can find a therapist using a therapist directory.

Many survivors report that they either contemplated or tried to leave their relationship several times before it finally ended. It is essential to set realistic expectations about how difficult leaving the relationship will be and how strong the urge to go back can be. Keep in mind that there is not a lot of research to suggest what amount of time or therapy will change the dynamics of the relationship; however, post-traumatic growth, recovery, and healing are possible.

Final Thoughts

The seven stages of trauma bonding show a repeated cycle of extreme highs and lows in abusive relationships, which often lead to the victim feeling isolated, lacking identity, and staying in the relationship for too long. However, breaking a trauma bond is possible, and support is readily available. In addition to forming a social support system and creating a safety plan, it is important to partner with a mental health professional who is highly trained and skilled in psychological abuse recovery. Otherwise, you may find a provider unfamiliar with the nature of abuse, which can create further confusion and be understandably triggering and retraumatizing. If you or a loved one is ready to get professional support, you can consult with a clinician to ensure they have the desired training to support your needs.

Erica VanEaton Healing
3h ·

With each speech I give and post I write, I explore the impact of my words and intentions. I consider the eyes and energy that are directed toward my family and others.
Is what I am sharing bringing an expansion of perception...and expression?
When we begin to ask these questions before we share ourselves with the world, it allows us to step into unity consciousnes. We become present and share our wisdom and visions rather than project our ideologies and beliefs.
Gifting others the space to do the same.

"I have learned silence from the talkative,

toleration from the intolerant,
and kindness from the unkind;
yet, strange, I am ungrateful to those teachers."
~Kahlil Gibran

<u>She Is Owning HerPeace</u>

nSetorosdp09675002g0li2701tllc1276ghmi8t10lthll u6ha0cgmagu5m ·

The narcissist doesn't find "a better person". They find someone who doesn't know better. Once you catch on to their lies, cheating, manipulation and gas lighting, they'll discard you and move on to the next one they've been grooming… OR, they'll move on from you because they have used you all up and you are of no value to them anymore. And they move on very quickly too. Not even 2-3 weeks go by after a break up and they're already in some form of a relationship. And I guarantee you they were grooming this person while in the relationship. And that's because they don't like to be by themselves. They can't. They don't like the thought of being by themselves, they're codependent upon other people. It's their "narcissistic supply". They need validation. They need to feel like the center of somebody's world, because ultimately, everything is and will always be about them. They are love bombing the new one, being on their best behavior and getting them trapped. They are portraying themselves as husband (or wife) material, loving, supportive, etc... and they are NOTHING like that. Nothing! They are literally the total opposite once they get you reeled in. They are highly arrogant, and believe they can do no wrong. They feel as if they're above the law and are better than everyone else. They are also jealous. They'll never be happy about your achievements or anyone else's except their own. Narcs pick certain people. They pick those who they know are caring, sweet, and nurturing. And trust me when I tell you, you have something they want. It might be money, it might be sex, or sometimes (if they live on their own) they'll move you in quickly so you can help them pay their bills while they drain you of your money and your soul. And they'll try to isolate you from friends and family in the long run. They won't want you to go anywhere, they'll want you to dress a certain way…and literally every single thing you do will become a problem. They're NEVER satisfied, and will ALWAYS have a void in their life that will never be filled. They're incapable of empathy, and understanding. The new person doesn't know what kind of hell they're getting into. They don't know they're getting ready to endure emotional abuse, mental abuse, and sometimes physical abuse. They'll literally make you feel like you're crazy and you're not. They'll even start arguments because it was a good day, and blame you for the argument they started, and tell everyone it's you that likes to argue. And they will disrespect you, talk down to you and about you, and devalue you. They also PURPOSELY provoke you so you can REACT (Reactive Abuse), so you can look like the crazy one. Because what happens is, they provoke you by yelling at you, being disrespectful, calling you out of your name, etc… but when you react to the disrespect, now they're the calm one, and you're irate, making YOU look crazy. They know how to play the game. Trust me. Narcissism is real. I could go on and on about narcissism. The best part is, I've been knowing now since seeking THERAPY thinking I was going crazy and that maybe I was part of the problem, smh. But now…I can spot it when I see it. Went through it damn near for the better part of my life, from relatives to "friends" to "partners" and the blindfold has come off.

There Are Three Mistakes You Should Never Make In Your Work Place

1. Never think your colleagues are your friends. They are not. They are just doing a job. When push comes to shove, they will save their skin and push you under the bus.

2. You should never reveal your personal life to your colleagues. Don't tell them your plans, your investments or your next big move. Only a fool reveals secrets.

3. When you disagree with company policy, never share it with any of your colleagues. Anything you share with your colleagues can and will be used against you.

If U can see it, U can achieve it!

Being in love makes you less of a productive person.

Allodoxaphobia - the fear of other people's opinions.

Surround yourself with people who are going to stimulate, inspire and lift you up. People who give and not take energy away from you. That's an energy drain. Get rid of anybody who drains your energy.

People change in 4 different Seasons when they hurt enough they have to, when they see enough they're inspired to, when they learn enough that they want to, when they receive enough that they're able to. Those are the 4 times that people change.

Eat, sleep, ground self and work on your own development and creativity. Listen to your own values, give yourself what you need, take care of yourself, give yourself your values before you decide to help other people or you become and feel like shit. Give people something to emulate that's sustainable.

The Ultimate Psychology Hack: read something aloud in the morning and at night 10X that you want to do and it will tell your body that you will accomplish it.

Positive, Peaceful & Filled With Love!

10 Stoic Quotes to Change Your Life in 2020

"Waste no more time arguing what a good man should be. Be One." — Marcus Aurelius

"It never ceases to amaze me: we all love ourselves more than other people, but care more about their opinion than our own." — Marcus Aurelius

"No great thing is created suddenly, any more than a bunch of grapes or a fig. If you tell me that you desire a fig, I answer that there must be time. Let it first blossom, then bear fruit, then ripen." — Epictetus

"It's not because things are difficult that we dare not venture. It's because we dare not venture that they are difficult." — Seneca

"You live as if you were destined to live forever, no thought of your frailty ever enters your head, of

how much time has already gone by, you take no heed. You squander time as if you drew from a full and abundant supply, though all the while that day which you bestow on some person or thing is perhaps your last." — Seneca

"You have power over your mind — not outside events. Realize this, and you will find strength." — Marcus Aurelius

"If you are pained by any external thing, it is not this thing that disturbs you, but your own judgment about it. And it is in your power to wipe out this judgment now." — Marcus Aurelius

"Difficulties strengthen the mind, as labor does the body." — Seneca

"Books are the training weights of the mind. They are very helpful, but it would be a bad mistake to suppose that one has made progress simply by having internalized their contents." — Epictetus

"Let us prepare our minds as if we'd come to the very end of life. Let us postpone nothing. Let us

balance life's books each day… The one who puts the finishing touches on their life each day is never short of time." — Marcus Aurelius

Ignorance & Ego vs. Higher Consciousness Utopian vs. Dystopian Society Become Spiritual & Operate Out of Higher Consciousness. There are two worlds: The Old Dystopian World vs. The World of The Gods.

1. Figure out 1 thing you want to accomplish. 2. What's the one action step daily that's going to get you to the accomplishment of that one thing? That's how you turn your life around.

In relationships you get what you deserve, you tolerate, what you encourage and what you reinforce. Guard your heart and start by setting boundaries and teach people how to treat you.

2 Things You Learn As You Get Older

1. You can make real friends with fake people.
2. You sit back and observe and realize that not everything needs a reaction.

Fly by the seat of your pants and don't worry about the outcome.

Your ability to create your dreams is your birthright. Raise your Vibration so you can attract what you want with more Inspiration.

You don't want to show weakness you want to show vulnerability which is courage so you can take steps necessary. Stand up and face that.

If you're the sort of King who can't stand the Fool then you're the tyrant. Develop your sense of humor: you don't get to decide what you think is funny for other people as that's not your judgement call. Things will not be a hell of a lot better because of your regulating what is and isn't funny.

When somebody says something and they pronounce it incorrectly don't correct that person as then it just derails the conversation and you should be focused on connecting with that person. Instead of correcting that person you should go

"You know what, Happy Valentine's Day to you, too".

THERE IS MORE WISDOM IN THE SUBSTANCE AND THE JOURNEY TO A DESTINATION THAN IT IS ACTUALLY REACHING THE DESTINATION. APPRECIATE THE ROUTE AND ALWAYS DO WHAT'S NECESSARY TO STAY WHERE YOU MADE IT TO. -RAY SCOTT

Somebody with empathy never loses themselves they stay contained. They are an individual. Well, an empath has no individuality. They are not a whole person. They become the other person.

"The Problem Is You Think You Have Time." – Buddha

memento mori: you're going to die: that is a fact!!!

Tourist dies while taking a selfie on Thailand's 'death railway'

How much does it cost to buy a horse and raffle the horse off for 25.00 a pop and that's your new job.

The whole system is about making as many people sick as possible w/ irradiated food, irradiated cigarettes, over 30,000 chemicals and preservatives added to the food supply not to mention spraying dangerous chemicals over crops that were used in WWII and I can't remember what the chemical was: it's not DDT as that was thought to be a wonder chemical to get rid of bugs. Then there's Big Pharma and every drug they invent from Nature that is programmed to make U sick w/ a new problem that needs to be treated, etc., adding "ethanol" to gas which will rot any plastic in your vehicle, the courts are corrupt as the day is longer, the Shadow Government is spraying at least 4 different kinds of chemicals in the air using aeroplanes (chemtrails), garbage is being dumped in the ocean, giant corporations pay members of Congress to not pass a bill that will help the planet heal, the "carbon tax" is designed to take more money out of your wallet, and the list of illicit things done by the Feds is too long to list here: that's just the beginning of the list. I'll just sit down and make a new list and write out how many illegal things are going on with this planet and then elaborate what is exactly happening all over w/ the Controlled Media: you get my points taken here??? Go ahead: add to this list: it just never stops. The System we now have is antiquated and corrupt to the core: why do U think Politicians love being Politicians??? I'm not going to say it...

Anonymous

Men have always had a say and it's typically to walk away taking no responsibility. Even when the man sticks around he still usually does little to nothing to help raise the child he helped make. Men keeping their mouth closed and pants on needs to happen.

Maverick Lover

Most men and women have "emotional problems" that complicate the pregnancy so both parties should use contraception or if they don't then a baby will be born unto this world: my mother got knocked up in 1962 and found a "surrogate nasty alcoholic step-father" to take care of my twin-sister and myself because my actual father Thomas P. Braine didn't want to take responsability for knocking her up as he was already married to "alcohol" and then she agreed to have one more child in exchange for him taking "responsability" for the two of us: it happens all the time: he took out most of his anger on me and my sister and I'm **THE Black Sheep** of the chaotic family, etc. So...that's all I can say: my mother was told by 5 doctors to "have an abortion" as she was only 5'3" tall and they were worried one of us twins wouldn't pull thru: we were born 1 month before the due date in August and had to be in an incubator like chickens are put in incubators to get the eggs to grow and hatch and we both survived. My sister came out 1st @ 3:17am and I was next 10 minutes later: got questions??? I can't make this stuff up.

EMPATH = feels things (but I usually don't listen to myself as I can't separate my sexual feelings from what people really want out of the ME, an

EMPATH). Narcissist = I can abuse U but U can't abuse me: it's all about **POWER & CONTROL** w/ the **Narcissist**. If your friend had any care for U he wouldn't tell U that he's an **EMPATH** as that's stuff that needs to be kept to oneself but I tend to tell people what's on my mind and I need a **BALL GAG** so that I don't do this: if your friend is being verbally/physically abusive with you then he's an abusive Narcissist who plays **POWER & CONTROL GAMES** with you: do U want a relationship like this??? I think not!!!

I'm a go getter: I go out, get what I need and bring it back to my place and enjoy it: I've had so much sex in my life that I need to stop doing and I also need to leave my nether regions alone as they get much too much attention: 4 days in a row is too much j.o. A man is only supposed to let the juice out 1X week according to Ayurvedic Healing: that's what I've heard and read online thru facebook. Is facebook even real??? Think about it: ME ME ME ME ME!

Does anybody know what the best kind of blow job is??? A bj with no teeth!

Never try to change another person unless they ask U for help or U make that suggestion: otherwise, you are wasting your time w/ that person.

<u>10 GREAT QUOTES ABOUT BEING SELF-MADE</u>
1. "The self is made, not given." – Unknown
2. "Winners are not born, they are self-made." – Pat Summitt
3. "I hate every minute of training. But I said, don't quit. Suffer now and live the rest of your life as a champion." – Muhammad Ali
4. "We are all self-made, but only the successful will admit it." – Earl Nightingale
5. "Inside every self-made man is a poor kid who followed his dreams." – Unknown
6. "Being self-made is a state of mind, and once you put that mentality to work, your success will come." - Dave East
7. "High expectations are the key to everything." – Sam Walton
8. "Being self-made means never making an excuse as to why you can't take steps toward whatever your goal is." – Nipsey Hussle

9. "We have the kind of self-made-man myth, which says that super-successful people did it themselves." – Malcolm Gladwell

10. "There is no such thing as a "self-made" man. We are made up of thousands of others. Everyone who has ever done a kind deed for us, or spoken one word of encouragement to us, has entered into the make-up of our character and of our thoughts, as well as our success." – George Matthew Adams

Bonus #1

"Talent wins games, but teamwork and intelligence win championships." – Michael Jordan

Bonus #2

"Surround yourself with people who lift you up. Your circle should want to see you win. Your circle should clap the loudest when you have good news. They should inspire you to push harder."

"Every master was once a disaster." Keep PUSHING forward.

P - Persistence

U - Until

S - Something

H - Happens!

Keep smiling and keep shining! Have a super powerful day!✨🌟💜🏆❕

Never try to change another person.
Here's why...
You really can't change another person — even if they're willing to change.
Trying to change another person is not only impossible but also signifies pride.
It means you're trying to claim a power beyond your comprehension and that's pride.
What we can do for a person who is working towards changing their selves is to help them.
We help them by offering resources, support, motivation e.t.c, to keep them on their journey.
That's all you can really do to help someone change.
Even when you help them, they still need a level of experience to get to a certain level.
From today, stop trying to change people.
If the change is really important to them and you want to help make it look attractive to them and watch them take the bait of change.
Like and share this post if you learned something from it.

If ur still looking thru a lens of inadequacy, judgment and insecurity that's a lie: cut yourself some slack!!! Be patient, loving, accepting, trusting. We are beneficiaries of life, not victims of it.

There's nothing wrong with you: keep saying it until it sinks in your beautiful brain: go now…

The women who lived as sex slaves to an Indian Goddess

To all the men I've p.o.'d off because I'm promoting a men's group as a way to create more healing in your life "I'm so sorry to have done that." This site can be a pain in the butt and I'm so sorry for my passive aggressive behavior. Thanks for your time: you are a beautiful person. Look up the words "trauma bonding" and then you'll know why you're addicted to anybody or anything: I know, I know: have a beautiful day when U get this massage!

6-year-old uses dad's phone to order nearly $1,000 of Grubhub across Michigan town

5 Losing relationship Strategies: Needing to be right, Controlling, Retaliation, Withdrawal, Unbridled self-expression Pat Trujillo

"Money may not be the most important thing in the world but it affects everything that is: affects your lifestyle, healthcare, your level of education, it affects everything on a day to day basis." Rich Dad, Poor Dad

The 5 Stages of The Modern Spiritual Awakening

1. Woke Stage: has to do with Oppression
2. Misunderstood: most people think they are misunderstood
3. The Dark Night of The Soul: You've lost your purpose
4. Enlightenment: Don't Think too Much or you'll lose your desire for sex, love & happeniss
5. Self-Re-Discovery: You re-discover what your true purpose in life is: to be U and to experience Nirvanna: the highest state of Consciousness

I DON'T HAVE A PERSONALITY DIS-ORDER I HAVE MENTAL DEFECTS AND A PERSONALITY THAT'S WAITING TO BURST WITH LIFE ALL OVER THE PLACE LIKE AN ORGASM!!!

LET'S DO IT!!!

1. Happiness is not the absence of problems. It's the ability to deal with them.
2. Feeling sad after making a decision doesn't mean it was the wrong decision.
3. You're not stressed because you're doing too much. You're stressed because you're doing too little of what makes U feel most alive.
4. The lesson you struggle with will repeat itself until you learn from it.

**Change Your Mind, Change Your Life –
Ashley A. Lenartson III**

Two laws: 1. Make people come to U 2. Use absence to create HONOR & RESPECT! Do it today…

Nanette Mary Michaud-Lenartson

Ashley Michaud-Lenartson, at Gene & Orlando's House, Portland, Maine Early 1990

Sharon on the lawn, Derby Kansas

**Ashley Michaud-Lenartson
Western Promenade**

Sharon-Rose Michaud-Lenartson

Eagle Lake Maine Lawn Homestead

Ashley Michaud-Lenartson, Eagle Lake Maine Lawn Homestead

Mickey Michaud-Lenartson, Eagle

Lake Maine Lawn Homestead

Ashley Michaue-Lenartson, 1981

**Ashley Michaud-Lenartson @ Jessica's
Home Portland, Maine**

**Ashley Michaud-Lenartson & Friends, Funtown/Splashtown, USA
Saco, Maine**

Nanette Mary Lenartson, Nani Girl

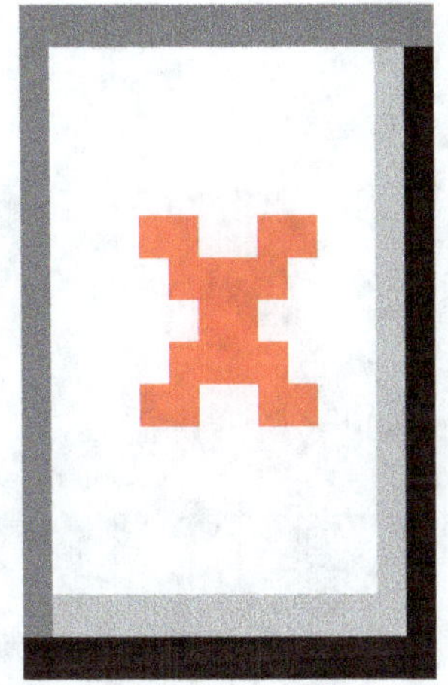

Ashley Michaud-Lenartson, Baxter Park, 1990's photo: Doug Palmer

Ashley Michaud-Lenartson, Donald's

Foster Home, Portland, Maine 1990's

Nanette, Rose & Carl Lenartson

**Carl Lenartson,
Nanette Lenartsons'
Brother**

Grandma Rose

Ashley-Albert, Sharon-Rose, Michael, Rose Filardi-Lenartson, Nanette (mom)

Mickey, Sharon & Ashley, New York City

**Rose Filardi's Husband,
Axel Lenartson**